NOT ON
YOUR
TINTYPE

To Tim,

*After beers in
Berlin, these
should be even
more fun!*

VOLUME I - INTRODUCTION

2008

ANDREW DANEMAN
COLLECTION OF
AMERICAN TINTYPES

ISBN 87-92135-00-5

Published by:
Northern Light Gallery Aps
Åkandevej 5
2700 Brønshøj
Danmark
Tlf. +45 3860 5942 • Fax +45 3881 5941

Further information available at:
www.not-on-your-tintype.com

Printed in Denmark by:
prinfodjurs
DJURS GRUPPEN A/S
Industrivej 18
8963 Auning
Tlf. +45 8648 3633 - Fax +45 8648 3408

Thanks –

To my wife Karen, first of all, for putting up all these years with all these little pictures. They take a lot of space, physically and emotionally and I know there have been times when she probably thought she came in a distant second behind them. That has never been the case.

To all the dealers and collectors since the '70s who have helped me and in some cases continue to help me find great images.

To you the reader, for taking in this first small view of my collection in the hope that it will entice you back for the next look.

TINTYPES

It is not my intention with this and the coming volumes to explain the Tintype in every aspect, historical and aesthetic. For this information I encourage the reader to study the more recent histories of photographic technique, though with an open mind. Traditionally writers have been biased against the Tintype as a process and unaware of its importance as an art form or cultural totem. The Tintype process has an important place in the history of photography, its period of use and proliferation second only to the negative/positive process, which is only just now waning in our digital age. In contrast to the negative/positive process, the instantaneous and inexpensive Tintype gave the American public a vehicle for acting out rituals psychological—stories famous, forgotten or perhaps known only to the tellers themselves—or for presenting themselves as part of the colorful fabric that was American society from 1856 through the end of the first world war.

Not on your Tintype
The origin and exact meaning of this phrase are still mysteries. Google searches turn up little. It seems to have been popular and popularly understood in the late 19th and early 20th centuries. Jack London used the phrase in his short story The Star Rover . Yet we still have no clue what it meant precisely. My research revealed possible meanings similar to "not on your life", "not on a stack of Bibles", "not on your mother's grave", or today's ubiquitous "no way!"

As demonstrated in many images in my collection, it became commonly understood that Tintypes offered a freedom to participants to go a little crazy. I believe most people knew that, beyond having a regular portrait made on these thin iron plates, there was also the possibility of letting loose and acting rather wild. Thus "Not on your Tintype" would still mean the equivalent of "no way" but from the understanding that "anything goes, but not that."

How it all began

On my birthday in 1975, my good friend John Reed Forsman gave me an Ambrotype as a present. Before then it never really occurred to me that one could own or would even want to own old photographs. I had become aware of antique images through the excellent Swiss publication *Camera*, but they struck me as something found in museum collections or books. That little Ambrotype portrait fascinated me, both for the person who once was and for the artifact in my hand. I began to explore the antique stores, flea markets and Photographica Fairs to see what else was available. There were lots of portraits in all techniques. Some were interesting, most weren't.

Why Tintypes, you ask? For me that answer is twofold, and the first part is easy. They were what a student married to another student could afford. You have to remember that the mortgage for a two-bedroom house in West Hollywood was $212 a month. We both worked throughout our student years, but paying $150-200 for an image was rarely possible. Then, as it still is now, great Tintypes cost only a fraction of the price of great Daguerreotypes or paper images. But, I soon began to wonder, were there even great Tintypes worth collecting? It quickly became clear to me that there was absolutely no shortage of ordinary ones.

The second part has to do largely with my taste as a maker as well as a collector of images. The best word to describe this is quirky. I am attracted to the off-beat, unusual, odd composition. I soon found the mode employed more often in Tintypes than any other photographic technique is perhaps as well described best as quirky. There seemed to be an abundance of these Tintypes, of people acting out dramas or being wild, silly, outrageous—similar to presentations we have learned to expect in later polaroids and snapshots. In its day this quirkiness was not only accepted but at a certain level expected of the posers for a Tintype. Maybe this was the commonly-understood meaning of the phrase "Not on your Tintype" that as far as one could go beyond the norm in being Tintyped, *that* was asking too much .

My first great discovery was an 1870s half-plate group of surveyors posed with all their equipment. It was hanging on the wall of a used furniture store on Western Ave. near Third St. in L.A., $15. It was like finding a gold nugget in a streambed and that solidified my decision to collect Tintypes showing groups of people.

While studying photography at Art Center College I began working for G. Ray Hawkins in his first gallery on Melrose. He suggested I pay a visit to Stephen White who had also recently opened a space near the Pacific Design Center, which I did. I worked at both these galleries for the next couple of years and was able to add to the collection with their help. However, Tintypes were definitely not their specialty and if I was going to get more than 25 images a year I needed to find other sources.

Then I discovered the art of trading. One day in 1977 I walked into a Pasadena antique store and bought a large collection of Western stereo views for 50¢ each. I had already begun subscribing to some of the xeroxed and printed photographica catalogues such as

Blueridge Photographics, RoBerta Etter and auctions such as Americana Arts in Maine and others. They all had a good supply of interesting Tintypes, but my growing hunger for them was threatening to break the bank. I asked Blueridge if they were interested in trading for the Western views and got a resounding, "yes", which resulted in the first bulk addition to the collection of 28 images.

Little by little from catalogues, photographica shows, flea markets, trades and private purchases I was beginning to get a sense of what the Tintype in America had been about and my love and appetite for them grew. By the early 1980s I was becoming known for this collecting interest as most collectors and dealers still despised Tintypes. One dealer selling a beautiful half-plate mourning portrait of a mother and daughters as an Ambrotype for $32.50 on hearing that it was actually a rare 1856 Griswold patent Tintype promptly reduced the price by $5.00. So it was for decades, Tintypes were considered the bottom of image collecting. This in fact was fine with me because it meant they stayed at the bottom of the price scale. The next 20 years witnessed many great finds, trades and purchases, but the greatest source was still to come.

ebay

On August 4, 1999 I joined ebay. I had heard a little about it but was skeptical about buying by auction on the internet. In fact my first purchase was not until December. With hundreds of images at a time changing constantly, it was the best source I had seen up to that point. The only problem was that being in Denmark and with the auctions' ending based on the Pacific Time Zone, it meant they ended typically in the middle of the night for me. In the beginning I won very few of the items because I was outbid in the last seconds even though I stayed up until 3 or 4 am to bid. Then I found out why- sniping - a service that executes bids for you at a specified number of seconds before the end. After that discovery my success rate in bidding changed from 10% to 90%. Since 2000 I have been buying an average of 10-15 Tintypes a month on ebay (see my feedback, tinman-i_am).

Vol. 1

For several years now I have wanted to present my Tintypes in book form, but couldn't decide on the format, first of all because there are so many interesting ones as well as the endless variations on the popular themes. For a long time I envisioned the volume as a thick coffee table edition with hundreds of illustrations and academic text; the ultimate book on American Tintype art. That project will never be possible for me to complete because each newly added Tintype or the ones yet to come prevent that.

Thus came the idea of doing a series. This format seemed ideal, since each in the series could be thematic, have different writers and need not be "complete or definitive". So here we are with number one in what I hope will be a long series of interesting images and texts. This introduction is however different than the ones I plan to follow. Rather than picking a theme for this number, I have decided to do a visual introduction to some of the themes and styles prevalent in American Tintypes from the start in 1856 and continuing in the 60 years that they flourished. Nor am I trying to include everything valuable or explain in one sitting the background, meaning and importance of the American Tintype.

In the subsequent volumes invited or volunteering authors will explore subjects such as staged and conceptual photography, identity, violence and affection, the artistic depiction of time, as well as work and leisure, life and death and much more. Another 50 Tintypes will augment each text. While I have images enough to make 50 volumes, I plan to produce 10.

The sequence of these Tintypes in volume 1 is explained after the plates. I hope you enjoy the journey and that it will encourage you to join me for volume 2.

Andrew Daneman
Copenhagen, 2007

1

2

3

4

5

6

7

8

9

10

11

12

13

14

15

16

17

18

19

21

20

21

22

22

23

23

24   *24*

25

26

27

28

29

30

31

32

33

34

35

36

38

39

40

41

42

43

44

45

46

47

48

49

50

51

52

1

KEY TO THE SEQUENCE

1. Poet surrounded by female admirers
2. Victim " " thieves threatening with guns
3. Pecurliar attire, mock indians " " knife
4. " " for Niagara Falls
5. Traveling by auto to " " , 4.5 horses
6. " " buckboard one horse power
7. Blacksmiths - " construction
8. " teamwork
9. " a romantic pose
10. Children with baskets, romantic pose
11. Boys pose " " of apples
12. Fullbody bobbing for "
13. Afloat in a washtub
14. Working a " and a broom
15. Armed with brooms and a rifle
16. " to kill, on an elephant
17. A world's fair, " " "
18. A country "
19. A crowded "
20. A " street
21. An empty " , small Tintype gallery
22. Large group in " " "
23. Musical " " " "
24. " serenade, on her knees
25. Pleading for him " " "
26. Hanging back to back
27. Youngsters " " "
28. Women entwined face to face
29. Two men "
30. Baby holding a man
31. Man " " baby
32. Arm " " "
33. Grabbing a woman's arm
34. " each other, whose arm?
35. Arm " his gold
36. Woman " watch from man
37. Man listening to his watch , friend makes a point
38. Woman " " her friends' discussion

39. An important point
40. Woman shows " her beau should kiss
41. Woman touching her "
42. " " " son
43. Three men "
44. Two " "
45. Fighting " having a game on the ground
46. Men playing checkers " " " (symmetrical pose)
47. Identical twins in checkered dresses " "
48. Men holding picture of sweetheart " "
49. Boys " " dad, drinking a toast
50. Men drinking on porch, face peers out of the window
51. Baby seated on couch, mom " " " shadow
52. " " " mother's lap, face scratched out
1. Poet and his female admirers, " " "

NOTES ON THE TINTYPES

1. CdV size. 1890s actual size
An unusually dramatic presentation of a poet and his enraptured fans. One woman's face has been scratched out. Previous writers suggested that this meant the person was dead, yet photographing the deceased was a common practice during the 19th century. It is my belief that the simpler, more direct explanation, that it was a face someone *didn't want to remember* that had been removed.

2. 7 X 5". 1880s actual size
A group of thugs, and these fellows look like the real thing. Those are probably their own weapons, not the photographer's props. They are relieving their victim of his wallet and watch.

3. CdV size. 1880s enlarged
Two not-so-convincing "savages".

4. CdV size. 1880s - 1890s actual size
These ladies' are dressed and equipped for a ride on the "Maid of the Mist" at Niagara Falls, though the falls are nowhere to be seen in this Tintype.

5. 4 X 5" size. 1900 actual size
Here before a gigantic painting of the falls, subjects could pose in the photographer's 1900 Stanley Locomobile - model "Milwaukee". This is clear because I have other Tintypes with the same car, the same painting but different people.

6. CdV size. 1890s enlarged
We modern viewers with an awareness of the symbols in comic strips, completely understand the "thought bubble" above the white horse, while the maker of this image never gave it a second thought.

7. Full plate size. 1880s actual size
A blacksmith shop, "Fred. Wagner & Brother" to be precise. To be less precise this could be any town in

the USA with dirt streets and brick/wood construction. It reminds us here that at one time each vehicle was a single, cooperative handmade project. Even the village rascals squeezed themselves onto the scene's right edge. The upper right corner shows us how delicate and damageable these thin metal plates really are. Bends are the worst, rust is supreme enemy number two.

8. CdV size. 1890s actual size

Blacksmiths hard a work on an axe head. This again shows how such production was a cooperative effort. These two could as easily be father and son as they could be Thor and Zeus.

9. 4X5" 1880s actual size

Blacksmiths once more, presented as romantic heroes, the heart-shaped light seems to focus on them like a spotlight.

10. 1/4 plate size. 1860s actual size

Three barefoot angels under soft tent light on a grassy floor. A summer day at a country fair with dad, whose leg we can make out to the right.

11. CdV size. 1890s actual size

At the same time scalawags and angels, these are the embodiment of the characters Mark Twain called Tom Sawyer and Huckleberry Finn.

12. CdV size. 1890s enlarged

People did so many mysterious things for their Tintype I find myself hoping that at the very least *they* knew what point they were trying to get across.

13. CdV size. 1890s enlarged

A patriotic group posed in a wooden tub. Before the advent of phone booths and Volkswagons for people stuffing, perhaps wash tubs served the purpose.

14. CdV size. 1890s actual size

Acceptable activities for women of that time were typically limited to cleaning, sewing and child care. Oddly, photography was an accepted female occupation.

15. CdV size. 1890s actual size

These women spoofing their male companion's weapon with brooms alludes to fighting their battles indoors.

16. CdV size. 1890s actual size

Hunting from atop a fake elephant and a little crowded it was.

17. CdV size. 1893 actual size

One could "see the world" in Chicago at the "White City" during the World's Fair in 1893 and there was a bit more room on a real elephant.

18. CdV size. 1890s actual size

A much smaller country fair gave locals a chance to meet, exchange recipes, sell livestock and bet on the horses sometimes.

19. CdV size. 1860s enlarged

Another local gathering with a big crowd, maybe at a fair as well but a balloon launching was a big attraction in the 1860s.

20. CdV size. 1880s actual size

Here we see in this small town everyone from within miles crowded into the view. The reason for this assembly and the faces are lost.

21. CdV size. 1870s enlarged

The photographer sits in the window of his tiny picture gallery, a boy poses jauntily in the street and a couple of others who happen to be nearby do not begin to fill this empty street . It is interesting how the structures in this and the previous image are nearly identical in their form, but is totally coincidental.

22. 9 X 11" 1880s actual size

This proud grouping of Improved Order of Red Men is jammed into a studio like the one in #21. Notice how the floor is mostly dirt with a walkway to the "staging area". This was likely to keep shoes from getting muddy if the dirt floor was a mess from outside conditions washing through.

23. 4 X 5" 1880s actual size

An equally crowded grouping as the previous, but at least in a more finished environment. This is probably a traveling Tintypist's studio, but could also just be a very small stationary studio.

24. CdV size. 1890s actual size

I would have expected the serenader to be on his knees and not the serenadee.

25. CdV size. 1890s actual size

Another story with most of the details left out. Who is the pleading woman, or the female vigilantes and what did he do? A plausible explanation is left to our own imagination.

26. CdV size. 1890s actual size

Hanging was not an uncommon motif in Tintypes so the next "logical" step was of course friends hanging together.

27. CdV size. 1890s actual size

This young couple seem to be at odds about something.

28. CdV size. 1890s actual size

Two women, sisters or friends, in a relaxed pose. During a period around 1890-1910 women began to wear ties and thus the heavy set woman at first glance appears to be a man.

29. CdV size. 1890s actual size

Two male buddies completely entangled - arms, legs, hands and the offer of a kiss, not something one sees too often in Tintypes.

30. CdV size. 1890s enlarged

This toddler holding a man in a most charming adult/baby depiction. The man, who may be the father or the grandfather, is most at ease with this energetic child.

31. CdV size. 1890s actual size

Not wishing to distract from the essence of the picture the fellow holding the child from behind the chair peeks around to see if the little one is centered.

32. CdV size. 1870s actual size

Most often photographers used a metal head clap for this purpose, but in this case a human clamp sufficed.

33. CdV size. 1890s actual size

All in good fun, we can surmise, because all three are smiling. The fellow grabbing her arm is telling her something, selling her something or just getting her to stop – shopping perhaps.

34. CdV size. 1890s actual size

These two fellows covered in fabric wearing odd hats are themselves strange enough. The inexplicable arm adds nothing to our understanding of this bizarre tale.

35. CdV size. 1890s enlarged

A much more understandable and goal-oriented arm relieves this oblivious daydreamer of his bag of gold. An unexpected effect, the arm materializing from thin air, is the result of a multi-image plate being trimmed wrong.

36. CdV size. 1900s enlarged

The man has taken the kneeling woman's watch. Little does he know, her friend is about to take it from him.

37. CdV size. 1870s actual size

The gent in the top hat listens to his pocket watch while his companion, finger raised, holds his own open watch.

38. CdV size. 1880s actual size

Two young women having a private, so they think, conversation while another listens in.

39. CdV size. 1860s actual size
This very serious discussion is partially explained by the scratched-on text, "Flour worth but $10.00".

40. Tintype button. 1890s enlarged
As he maneuvers past this young damsel's hat, she makes it clear he has not yet earned access to her lips.

41. CdV size. 1890s enlarged
Another young lady showing how easy it is to control a young man with only one finger. They wear matching shiny outfits which give the impression of stage costumes or band uniforms.

42. CdV size. 1880s actual size
The fragile connection this mother attempts to preserve is not returned by the young man. While it is not a full-blown "cold shoulder" he gives her, he attempts to maintain separation.

43. CdV size. 1890s actual size
Three men out painting the town and about to change their orientation from vertical to horizontal.

44. CdV size. 1890s actual size
Boxing was a very common presentation of male contact in Tintypes.

45. Quarter plate. 1861-4 enlarged
Union soldiers having a game of poker on the ground. They all show their hands *and* weapons. There must have been some controversy as they are all showing straights or flushes!

46. CdV size. 1890s enlarged
More likely a coincidence than a planned composition, the symmetry of this image is perfect none-the-less.

47. Quarter plate. 1860s enlarged
Twins in checkered dresses offers one of only *two* possibilities in presenting identical twins; either as a mirror image or *not*. Subtleties of posture and expression prove they are individuals.

48. Sixth plate. 1860s actual size
Pictures of their sweethearts confirm that these men longed for their loved ones however far apart they found themselves.

49. 4 X 5". 1880s actual size
Again a picture within a picture serves to illustrate the thoughts of these young men, toasting dad, either still in the "old country" or at peace in the "ever after".

50. CdV size. 1890s enlarged
The 3 fellows posed on this porch are not quite as interesting as the mysterious person peering out of the window behind them.

51. CdV size. 1880s enlarged
The toddler has not yet decided how to take this whole experience, but at least mom though not completely in the picture is still near by.

52. CdV size. 1890s enlarged
It is most likely a hostile action that led to this facial retouching, because the effect is clearly visible on the reverse as well!

1. CdV size. 1890s actual size
We have now come full circle and are still wondering what this woman might have done to deserve such treatment.

TINTYPE SIZES

Oversize . . .	typically 8 X 10" - 11 X 14"
Full or Whole plate	6 1/2" X 8 1/2"
no plate name	5 X 7"
Half plate	.4 1/4 X 5 1/2"
some half plates	4 X 5"
Quater plate	.3 1/4 X 4 1/4"
Carte de Visite	3 1/2 X 2 1/2"
Sixth plate (standard)	.3 1/4 X 2 3/4"
Ninth plate (standard)	2 1/2 X 2"
Gem	1 1/2 X 1"
Stereo	
(on one plate)	3 1/2 X 7"
(as two images side by side) . . .3 1/2 X 2 1/2"	

Images from multiplying cameras vary depending on the size of the plate and the number of multiple images on that plate.

There an be 4, 6, 8, 9, 12 or 16 almost identical images depending on the combination mentioned above.

Further information available at:
www.not-on-your-tintype.com